A Cowboy Dev

How Faith, Hope & Love
Made a Rodeo Family

The Harris Family

Printed in The United States of America

ISBN-978-0-578-53625-5

May YOUR days be filled with moments that
Capture YOUR soul and YOU create memories
that last a lifetime

May YOU have the eyes of a Noticer and the
perspective to become a better version of
Yourself.

Blessings of love, laugher, health & happiness;
From our home to Yours

The closer YOU walk with the Lord, the easier
it is to trust that his word is true and never
changes.

A special thank you to our Photographer, Mrs. Tiffany Baird for the cover and photos throughout this book. You and your family are a blessing to our Rodeo Family. Thank you for sharing the love, laughter, tears and memories.

Thank you for capturing what the heart sees!

Proverbs 27:23-27 NKJV
"23 Be diligent to know the state of your flocks, and attend to your herds;
24 For Riches are not forever, nor does a crown endure to all generations.
25When the hay is removed, and the tender grass shows itself, and the herbs of the mountains are gathered in,
26 The lambs will provide your clothing, and the goats the price of a field.
27 You shall have enough goats milk for your food, for the good of your household and the nourishment of your maidservants."

About the Authors

This devotional will give you insight to one family's walk in faith and inspire you through real life, genuine stories of their trials, God's love and answered prayers.

The Harris family is lead by Scott and Shelenea Harris who have been married for 20 years. They have seven children and one grandchild. This homeschooling, rodeo family is devoted to sharing their stories of God's hand at work in their lives.

For over seven years they have participated in the Virginia High School Rodeo Association. Rodeo is a family sport that compliments their lifestyle of hard work and faith in God. The wins and losses they have endured through this great sport have only brought them closer as a family and allowed them to experience God. Join them on their wildest adventures filled with laughter, tears and humbling experiences through A Cowboy Devotional.

Jacob, Anna & Matthew have all served on the Cinch Team which recognizes those who excel in academic and athletic performance. Jacob served as then Student Vice President and is a 7x National Qualifier, finishing in the top 20 in Chute Dogging and Bull Riding. He has competed in Bull Riding, Chute Dogging, Tie Down, Team Roping, Light Rifle and Trap.

Anna has served as the Student Ambassador and is a 4x National Qualifier. She has competed in Barrel Racing, Pole Bending, Goat Tying, Ribbon Roping, Light Riffle and The Queens Contest.

Matthew currently serves as the Student Ambassador and is a 2x National Qualifier. He has competed in Bull Riding, Team Roping, Ribbon Roping, Goat Tying and Light Rifle.

Emily competes in the Maverick Division of the Virginia Junior High School Rodeo Association.

Delanie and Elizabeth are eagerly awaiting their turn to team rope together.

Table of Contents

Dedication

We would like to dedicate this book to all of our readers and the legacy they share with others.

Timothy 4:12 NKJV 12 "Let no one despise your youth, but be an example to the believers in word, in conduct, in love, in spirit, in faith, in purity."

If I could give one word of advice to our upcoming cowboys it would be to embrace every moment in life, and strive to become someone that you will be proud of later in life. Don't be too proud to ask for help and give help without hesitation. The same person asking for your help today will be there for you in your time of need; just like the neighbors I helped who offered their time in building our barn. How we treat people matters. In fact, I believe having respect and decency for others is the most important thing we can do in this life.

Luke 12:48 says, "To whom much is given, much will be required".

I believe we are held responsible for how we utilize what we are given and will do my best to uphold the Cowboy Code. ~Jacob Harris

Preface

We would be cheating you out of an amazing story if we didn't start from the beginning and show you through our words and life exactly how amazing God truly is. Upon writing this devotion, and looking back, we see that God was directing our path --leading the way the entire time.

It is remarkable the people that God handpicked and placed in our lives over the course of this journey -- all in His perfect timing. Some people have come and gone, only here for the short leg of the journey. While others we somehow know will be with us for a lifetime.

This has been an adventure that we have not taken lightly. We have discovered that the very prayers we were praying and the actions we were taking based on God's wisdom and guidance (even in the hardest times and when it didn't make sense), that God really was moving mountains and making a way. He often uses ordinary people like our family and yours to accomplish His will, even while still giving us all freedom of choosing. He can take what we have and add the increase if we are willing to trust Him with the reins and follow His lead.

"You did not choose Me, but I chose you and appointed you that you should go and bear fruit, and that your fruit should remain, that whatever you ask the Father in My name He may give you." John 15:16 (New King James Version)

Day 1

Ride Bulls and Tell Them About Jesus

"Mama, I need a set of spurs." In a split second several questions like, "How do you even know what spurs are?" ran through my mind. "Absolutely not. You will get hurt." What mother in her right mind buys her three year old son spurs? "Oh and Mama, I don't want plastic ones. I want real spurs." "Matthew honey, you do not need spurs." "Mama, I want to ride bulls and tell people about Jesus."

There are many lessons to motherhood that I have yet to learn, but I know that you do not dispute Jesus. "Son, I will google where we can buy a pair." I must confess, it took me a while to take all this in. We did not have any livestock. No cows or horses, just chickens, but this is where our rodeo journey begins.

Jeremiah 29:11 NKJV 11 "For I know the thoughts that I think toward you, says the Lord, thoughts of peace and not of evil, to give you a future and a hope." One little boys dream lead to their family's legacy.

Day 2

Load the Chute

Looking back it seems surreal how we got to where we are today. I know I will miss a few details but I want to show you exactly how "God truly is in it." It came with struggles, laughter, tears and often times, pure disbelief. From a little boy that wanted spurs so he could tell people about Jesus to A Rodeo Family that became our Legacy.

Walking around Tractor-Supply, Matthew spotted a guy with a bull-riding buckle. Not afraid to ask questions, Matthew struck up conversation about his buckle and how he could get one of his own. We learned that this guy's name was McGee and he was heading to a bull riding clinic the next weekend. Before I knew it, this mama, pregnant with baby number six, was loading the van heading to Maryland for a Bull Riding clinic while daddy stayed home to work.

Upon our arrival and I shamefully admit this; I told the kids, "If I say get in the van, don't ask questions and do as I say." There was only one woman and a lot of guys. I won't lie, at first glance, they looked rough. Some of them had been there the night before, slept in their trucks and camped out. I found out that this is their way of life. Soon it would become ours.

Being a mama is something I pride myself in. Making sure my babies are tended to is my lifelong commitment. As we sat there on the ground and these strangers helped Matthew put his spurs on right and talked to him about what 'mutton bustin' was, I felt so much peace. These young men had nothing to gain from us but were willing to give their time and wisdom.

Matthew 7:1-2 NKJV "Judge not, that you be not judged. 2 For with what judgment you judge, you will be judged; and with the measure you use, it will be measured back to you.

When I called home to tell Scott that I had spent the day with some of the most amazing, go out of their way to help you people, he was relieved. I told him how I felt horrible because I had judged them before I knew anything about them. Our family would have missed a life changing moment if I had not trusted that God led us there for a reason.

Proverbs 3:5-6 NKJV "Trust in the Lord with all your heart,
And lean not on your own understanding;
6 In all your ways acknowledge Him,
And He shall direct your paths."

"I was shivery before, then after I was sweaty." ~Matthew Harris age 4 his first sheep ride.

Day 3
Support Your Brother

With Matthew's sheep riding a success, day three of the clinic consisted of calf and miniature bull riding. This entire trip had been planned for Matthew, his bull riding and him telling people about Jesus.

Matthew absolutely loved the mutton bustin', but was a little skeptical about the calf riding. He stood back and watched a few of the other boys ride. Even though Jacob, Matthew's older brother, had not paid, they asked him if he'd like to try. Just as I expected, Jacob said, "No thank you." Jacob was quiet, shy and somewhat a recluse. To be blunt, he also lacked self confidence.

I was brought up that we are family and family helps one another to become their very best. I had seen those miniature bulls and they really had not caused any harm. Like any good mother would do I simply walked over to Jacob and told him to get on that bull and ride it one time to support his brother and show him it was safe. Jacob agreed to do just that.

In the blink of an eye he was on a bucking dummy, getting a crash course in bull riding. As promised, these fellas were right by his side, coaching him the entire way. However, the outcome was not as expected.

Jacob rode that bull for 8 seconds and his life was changed forever. It truly is a sport that you either love it, and are all in, or it just isn't your thing. To say the least, it definitely was his thing. He climbed down into the chute on every bull they offered him. He was "hooked" as they call it.

Both boys had the bull riding fever and we had no idea how our lives were about to be changed, forever. Our search for a rodeo began.

Jeremiah 29:13 NKJV 13" And you will seek Me and find Me, when you search for Me with all your heart."

Day 4

So It Begins

It is amazing the power of social media. With one inquiry, an old high school friend, Keli, got us all the contact information we needed. In no time we were learning about call-ins, button up shirts, dress codes, rodeo gear and our soon to be forever home and family, The Virginia High School Rodeo Association.

We were informed that the association had gear that we could borrow until we learned more about what we needed and if this was really our thing. From day one our family was in awe of how everyone helped each other. I thought I would never learn the difference between the two redheaded strangers, Tina and Misty; that have become the best of my friends and like another mother to my children.

When I woke up at daybreak, parked in someone's pasture, in the middle of nowhere, I stepped out of our 1988 Nomad camper and saw kids tending to their horses, brushing them down, packing water buckets, and carrying hay. I somehow knew we were exactly where we needed to be. As I made my way to the port a john, I thanked God for getting us here.

I saw kids taking initiative, showing respect to The American Flag, The Cowboy Prayer and The National Anthem. I heard, "Yes Ma'am" and "No Sir's". They even had Cowboy church every Sunday. This is exactly what we wanted instilled in our kids.

We started at the beginning of the second half of the season and it was an incredible experience for all of us. Our entire family managed to get involved, helping in some way. The season ended like it always does; a pot luck dinner, cowboy prom and the Award Ceremony. Matthew was the 2012 Reserve Mutton Bustin' Champion and Jacob became the 2012 Jr. High Bull Riding Champion for the state of Virginia.

If there ever was a place that felt like home and family no matter where it was, this was it. It is important to look out for one another and surround yourself with people willing to do the same.

Philippians 2:1-3 NKJV "Therefore if there is any consolation in Christ, if any comfort of love, if any fellowship of the Spirit, if any affection and mercy, 2 fulfill my joy by being like-minded, having the same love, being of one accord, of one mind. 3 Let nothing be done through selfish ambition or conceit, but in lowliness of mind let each esteem others better than himself. 4 Let each of you look out not only for his own interests, but also for the interests of others."

Day 5

All Good Things Must Come to an End

I always wondered about this saying, "All good things must come to an end." We had just come back from one of the most amazing experiences of our lives. Our family had stepped out of our comfort zone, took a leap of faith and simply trusted God. The kids had overcome learning a new sport, making call-ins, helping people as they learned, made new friends and the boys had won their first buckles. There was only one problem; our girls.

The girls had watched their new friends compete in the all the rodeo events: Barrel Racing, Pole Bending, Goat Tying, Team Roping, Tie-Down, Chute Doggin', Break-Away, Bare Back and Bronc Riding and watched as their brothers proudly took their seat on the sheep and bulls. We watched our boys in the arena and our girls on the sidelines running a horseless barrel pattern. Our hearts broke as parents because if we could get a horse, we did not have the means to keep or transport one. It was not fair to our girls to watch our boys compete while they chased make believe cans. We were doing all that we could, giving our kids our very best, but it just wasn't enough. We fell short.

That evening as our family gathered in the living room, through tear filled eyes and a clutched throat I broke the news to them. "I know that we have had the best time ever. Your dad and I are so proud of you boys, but we cannot do another season." No one spoke, but the room was not silent. You could hear the sobbing and as I looked at my husband, I knew his heart was as broken as anyone else's.

Now mind you, I am saying this to kids that worked together planning bake sales, collecting pop cans and picking up every piece of scrap metal they could find. All five kids worked together knowing that only the two boys would be able to compete in the rodeo.

We had spent countless hours in the freezing cold and hot as can be weather at practice pens and rodeos. Our family started taking more road trips and I had learned how much help a rodeo family would be to pretty much anyone they encountered. We had miles of laughter chasing those white lines. We shared more meals and cookouts than we ever had in our life. It was Heaven sent. Nonetheless, we couldn't do for our boys and not do for our girls.

"I know you all love it, but boy's, it simply is not fair to the girls. We have no way of letting them compete. We don't have a horse." As the boys understandingly shook their head, Anna was the first to speak. "Mama, if me not getting to barrel race means that the boys have to quit rodeo, I am fine just going and being with everyone. I don't have to compete, but I don't want to not go to the rodeos anymore. We have so much fun and have made many new friends."

The tears fell harder and the sobs grew realizing that this eight year old sister would not only work hard to help her brothers reach their dreams, but would sacrifice her own so they didn't have to. This spoke volumes about her character and the impact rodeo had on our lives. In that moment our bond as a family grew stronger, with many more to follow.

Luke 9:24 NKJV 24 "For whoever desires to save his life will lose it, but whoever loses his life for My sake will save it."

Day 6

Forever Changed

Something life changing was happening in our family. Prayers became more sincere. Our dreams grew bigger and had more life to them. We had been forever changed. It was not one thing in particular that stood out but everything wrapped up into one. We shared meals, took road trips, got lost, found our way, had mishaps, amazing experiences, losses, and championships. There were close calls, emergency room visits and prayers from one friend to another. It's crazy how one's needs were recognized and many pitched in to help before asked. Life long bonds were made, not just between friends but within our family. We had one another's back no matter what the need was. We watched dreams come true and as dreams were given up. Funny how the struggles and scariest moments bring out the best you have to offer.

Imagine thirty or more families looking out for one another, sharing a common ground. It's not about being better than anybody but helping people be the best they can be. Kids share horses, clothes, tack and whatever it takes to get them to the rodeo and through the alley way with the most successful run possible. No one goes hungry, does without, is left behind or on the side of the road. It puts me in the mind of the scripture in Matthew 6:31-33 NKJV 31 "Therefore do not worry, saying, 'What shall we eat?' or 'What shall we drink?' or 'What shall we wear?' 32 For after all these things the Gentiles seek. For your heavenly Father knows that you need all these things. 33 But seek first the kingdom of God and His righteousness, and all these things shall be added to you.

Actions speak louder than words and it says a lot when a group of people come together to bring out the best in one another. We share in one another's life, adventures and defining moments. Where one lacks, the other leads. I believe everyone has to find their place in this world. A place to fit in and call home, and for us, we found our place in the Rodeo.

I have always said I didn't want the village raising my kids, but if that village happens to be the Rodeo Family, I will take it.

John 14:2-4 NKJV 2 " In My Father's house are many mansions; if it were not so, I would have told you. I go to prepare a place for you. 3 And if I go and prepare a place for you, I will come again and receive you to Myself; that where I am, there you may be also. 4 And where I go you know, and the way you know."

Day 7

God's Timing

"Lord, if you don't want us in the rodeo, remove it from our lives." It was that plain and simple. I did not want our family to be where God didn't want us. "Lord, You know me and that you have to make it clear, very clear." As the sun broke the darkness, the ring of the phone broke the silence.

"Hello. Yes we will be home all day. It would be wonderful to see you all. Wow. Are you serious? That would be amazing. Are you sure? Have a safe trip and we will see you soon."

"Wow. God you are amazing, right on time." I don't know what I was most excited about, the surprise, or that God had just made himself perfectly clear.

We had known the Nelson's for a couple years now. They had become our family, but most important they became our mentors. We call on them in times of prayer and rejoicing. On more than one occasion, they taught us about being obedient to the Lord.

Now I don't know about what takes place at your house when you know company is going to show up, but at The Harris House, we bake a batch of brownies and do a speed cleaning. I told the kids that the Cowboy Preacher, Mike Nelson and his wife, Diane was taking a Sunday drive and heading our way.

A couple hours later as the Nelson's pulled in the driveway, the looks on everyone's faces was priceless. God's timing is everything. We did not have a horse or a place to keep one but we had just been delivered a horse trailer. It was not the fanciest but it was an answered prayer.

As I explained to everyone how Mr. Nelson's phone call had broken the silence of my morning prayer, he explained how God had awoken him that very morning and told him to bring our family that horse trailer. To Mike and Diane, it was a beat up horse trailer. To our family, it was hope

Romans 15:13 NKJV 13 "Now may the God of hope fill you with all joy and peace in believing, that you may abound in hope by the power of the Holy Spirit."

Day 8

The Land

Photo Credit: "Pop's" Joe Smith

We didn't know how, but we knew that God had just delivered us a horse trailer and surely he wouldn't deliver a horse trailer if he did not intend on providing the horse. We lacked the understanding, but we were growing in our faith. Our horse skills were as limited as the pasture we had. I was reminded of and reread one of our family's favorite stories, 'Where the Red Fern Grows.' I spoke to the Lord, "If you don't want us in the rodeo, remove it from our lives." It was that plain and simple. I did not want our family to be where God didn't want us. "Lord, you know me and that you have to make it clear, very clear."

I asked the kids if they were willing to meet God halfway. They agreed and just like circling the walls of Jericho, the kids and I marched around our property. We stopped at the edge of the land beside our home, placed our hands right there on the ground and asked God that if it was his will, that he make a way.

We continued to save money and trust God for His word. To our amazement, the land owner contacted us giving us the first option to buy. This was the first time we had ever seen, heard from or even knew who the owner was. As circumstance would have it and never like we plan, the land became ours. As always, God revealed His goodness and faithfulness to our family.

Hebrews 11:1 NKJV "Now, faith is the substance of things hoped for, the evidence of things not seen."

Day 9

Building Fences

One of the greatest things that ever happened in our household was the day we needed to build a fence. We had the land, now we needed a fence to provide a safe pasture for what at times still seemed impossible, a horse. It was the start of winter, my husband was working a lot of hours at the mill and I just had a baby.   This left the three oldest children who still lived at home, Jacob age 13, Anna 11 and Matthew 9 at the time to fence in the 4.5 acre field. Having a newborn, a two and four year old, my place was in the home and I could only watch out the window as production began.

They were making pretty good progress and had made it down over the knoll so I didn't see my two boys burying my daughter, Anna in one of the post holes. Your typical post hole is at least two feet deep.

Along about supper time the boys thought Anna could get out, so they loaded the truck up and left her there in the bottom of the field. A little after the two culprits came in, washed up and sat down to eat, I noticed Anna was not with them. When asked where she was, the looks on their face told me something was not as it should be. They assumed that since she was only buried to her waist in a post hole that she could get out easy. Needless to say I was not happy. I sent them right back down there to get her out of the hole. Afterwards I kept a check on them and I am pleased to report that no further incidents occurred that day.

Post holes needed dug, 114 to be exact. After about 50, The Towery Family brought their tractor and dug the back side of the holes. If you have ever used a set of posthole diggers you realize what a blessing this was. Our neighbor came and dug a few holes for us as well. It was hard labor but the kids proved themselves that they were willing to put forth the effort. The challenges they faced completing this job prepared them for the next.

Watching the kids work together, listening to them talk, make plans adjustments, figuring materials and prices, filled my heart.

The kids also had arguments, disagreements and I realized that I had to stay out of it. Respect among them grew as they learned to work with and for one another. They had a common goal and knew that the completion depended on them.

From this moment on, I knew that anytime they needed to bond I would let them build a fence or work on a hard, almost seems impossible to complete job. All too often we want to make it easy for our kids, do it for them because we know how or can offer some help. Truth is we rob them of 'self-satisfaction' and the realization that they can do hard things, successfully. There is something to be said about someone, especially a child who faces adversity with confidence.

Matthew 7:24-27 NKJV 24 "Therefore whoever hears these sayings of Mine, and does them, I will liken him to a wise man who built his house on the rock: 25 and the rain descended, the floods came, and the winds blew and beat on that house; and it did not fall, for it was founded on the rock."
26 "But everyone who hears these sayings of Mine, and does not do them, will be like a foolish man who built his house on the sand:27 and the rain descended, the floods came, and the winds blew and beat on that house; and it fell. And great was its fall."

Day 10

The Horse

Written by: Anna Harris

Ever since I was a little girl I have loved, admired and wanted a horse. Any time a birthday or Christmas came around my mom and dad would ask, "What do you want, besides a pony?" The real horse business was slow so I asked for the next best thing, an outdoor, spring loaded, rocking horse.

As soon as Black Lightning was unboxed, I was riding like the wind. We were the fastest team since Hidalgo and Frank Hopkins. Lightening and I never lost a race. We became famous and I decided to become sheriff, always being merciful to the bad guys. We were the first lady and horse rider to win a race of men only at age 6. It is amazing all the adventures a young girl's imagination can take her on.

One morning my mother woke my siblings and myself. She asked, "Do you believe God will bless you with a horse?" By that time my horse fever had spread, so everybody stepped forward and said, "Yes ma'am." We walked around the pasture we wanted and prayed. When we came back around we laid hands on the land and said, "This land is ours." We began saving our money and a few months later, that exact property went up for sale. We bought it as fast as the Road Runner being chased by Wile E Coyote.

My brother's and I, with some help, built a fence and we got our first horse. What's amazing about it is that we brought Roy home two days before Christmas! We had to work with him to load into our small trailer and teach him to walk through our basement doors. Yes you read that right. You see, your livestock needs to have trees or a shed where they can have a safe shelter.

When it was cold at night, Good Ol' Roy had to duck his head and walk through the French doors leading into our basement. Imagine dad's surprise when he pulled up one night after work and had a horse staring through the door at him. We had not built a run in shed yet so all winter long our posh pony spent the chilly nights in our basement cozy as can be.

I learned that you have to wait for good things to come your way. God will bless you in the right time.

Psalm 27:14 NKJV "Wait on the Lord; Be of good courage, And He shall strengthen your heart; Wait, I say, on the Lord!"

Day 11

The Barn

Written by: Jacob Harris

We often don't take time to recognize when the Lord has been at work in our lives. We get so caught up in what we are doing, supposed to do, and have done that we take for granted the little things we are blessed with. A few winters back, dad and I decided to start construction on our barn. The planning and funding was up to him and the construction was up to me. I was thirteen at the time and although I was pretty handy, my carpentry skills could have used a little work, if you know what I mean.

This is where another little blessing came into play. Our neighbor drove over to the house and offered to drill the holes for our 16 foot six by six to go in the ground. Drilling began on a Friday so dad could be home for this part of the process. After the twelve posts were set and while taking a break over a glass of sweet tea, our neighbor offered to help us build the barn.

My neighbor and I worked side-by-side through freezing rain, sleet, and snow. Dad would come home and on the weekends and all three of us would work on the barn together. It took about three months working around weather and tight schedules for us to finish the barn. Now every time I wake up I'm reminded that the Lord has blessed me in more ways than I can ever imagine.

Finally we had the barn we prayed for and I had learned just enough carpentry to get me in trouble! I am thankful for the skills and wisdom that were handed down to me one nail at a time.

Proverbs 3:10-20 NKJV 10" So your barns will be filled with plenty, And your vats will overflow with new wine. 11 My son, do not despise the chastening of the Lord, Nor detest His correction; 12 For whom the Lord loves He corrects, Just as a father the son in whom he delights. 13 Happy is the man who finds wisdom, And the man who gains understanding; 14 For her proceeds are better than the profits of silver, And her gain than fine gold. 15 She is more precious than rubies, And all the things you may desire cannot compare with her. 16 Length of days is in her right hand, In her left hand riches and honor. 17 Her ways are ways of pleasantness, And all her paths are peace. 18 She is a tree of life to those who take hold of her, And happy are all who retain her. 19 The Lord by wisdom founded the earth; By understanding He established the heavens; 20 By His knowledge the depths were broken up, And the clouds drop down the dew."

Day 12

My Brother and I

Written by Matthew Harris

My brother and I have been roping for three years now but we have only roped with each other once. The organization we usually rope for, The Virginia High School Rodeo, is divided into three groups. Unfortunately we are in separate divisions, so when we got the chance to compete in a professional circuit together we were more than eager to give it a try.

I have a confession, there are only a select few people that I can rope with without being nervous and that also depends on the arena. So here I was at my first professional rodeo waiting in the holding pen without a single drop of fear.

Just a little background of myself. As a former steer rider, adrenaline is like a necessity. Adrenaline is normally caused by fear, but as I sat there looking at the hipbone of that steer, waiting for Jacob to nod, all that was on that horse was a pumped twelve year old little brother ready to get it done on the heel side.

Well if you ask my friends, they will tell you I snagged the outside leg, while slipping the left leg. To simplify that, I just caught one leg, which gave us a five second penalty. That gave us a 13 second run, one of my best.

With all things considered, it was an awesome rodeo. The thing is there is a connection in brothers that fuels knowledge about each other that no one else knows and that creates an unbreakable bond and compatibility.

Psalm 133:1-3 KJV 133 "Behold, how good and how pleasant it is for brethren to dwell together in unity!

2 It is like the precious ointment upon the head, that ran down upon the beard, even Aaron's beard: that went down to the skirts of his garments;

3 As the dew of Hermon, and as the dew that descended upon the mountains of Zion: for there the Lord commanded the blessing, even life forevermore."

Day 13

Horsemanship

Written by: Jacob Harris

When I think of horsemanship, the first thing that comes to mind is friendship, respect, and trust. Without these three main character traits there is no way anyone can possibly expect to be a true horseman. In order to become one with your horse you have to build a bond. His trust has to be earned and the only way for that to happen is to listen to him. "Every time I say this people look at me like I have two heads, but it's true." Horses are constantly sending and receiving signals. All you have to do is listen; not with your ears, but with your eyes. Paying attention to the small changes in body position and breathing patterns have saved my hind end more than once.

Something that I really like about working with horses is that there is always room for improvement. No matter how much I think I know, there is someone to learn from. There is a small piece of knowledge to be gained, Even if it's just watching and learning from other people's mistakes,

If given the opportunity to train horses for a living I would smile and say that would be great. When I am with the horses, watching them learn to use the thinking side of their brain it makes me feel like I have helped them reach a new level in their lives. I have helped create a functional tool that is not only used to work but is also the most trustworthy companion. Horses are not like people, they do not strive to outdo their neighbor, they cannot be bribed, they never lie, and most important they strive to be with you just as much if not more than you want to be with them.

Proverbs 3:5-18 NKJV
5 Trust in the Lord with all your heart,
And lean not on your own understanding;
6 In all your ways acknowledge Him,
And He shall direct your paths.
7 Do not be wise in your own eyes;
Fear the Lord and depart from evil.
8 It will be health to your flesh,
And strength to your bones.
9 Honor the Lord with your possessions,
And with the first fruits of all your increase;
10 So your barns will be filled with plenty,
And your vats will overflow with new wine.

11 My son, do not despise the chastening of
the Lord,
Nor detest His correction;
12 For whom the Lord loves He corrects,
Just as a father the son in whom he delights.
13 Happy is the man who finds wisdom,
And the man who gains understanding;
14 For her proceeds are better than the profit
of silver,
And her gain than fine gold.
15 She is more precious than rubies,
And all the things you may desire cannot
compare with her.
16 Length of days is in her right hand,
In her left hand riches and honor.
17 Her ways are ways of pleasantness,
And all her paths are peace.
18 She is a tree of life to those who take hold
of her,
And happy are all who retain her.

Day 14

Good Character

It is important to realize the influence you have on others and them on you. We have all heard, "Show me your friends and I will show you your future!" Your life will be an example of, who you break bread, run and spend the most time with.   You can judge a man by the company he keeps.

It has been eight years now since I realized that God had answered one of my most important prayers. "Lord, surround my family with good, like minded, God fearing, hard working, people. Lord, give my children friends who will bring out their best, and parents that look out for all the kids."

As I type this I am in tears because God done that very thing. He placed us in the center of this Rodeo Life that is like no other. He answered this Mama's prayer.

Parents I cannot express to you enough the importance of who you surround yourself, your family and your children with. It matters! God hears your prayers. It is worth the effort you put into it. Keep praying and following God's nudges. Looking back, I see how God's grace and mercy changed our lives. It is amazing how he takes care of us when we seek him.

1 Corinthians 15:33 NKJV "33 Do not be mislead: "Bad company corrupts good character."

I encourage you to write out your prayer concerning the character you want circled around your family. Be mindful of what you are doing and where you are spending your time.

Day 15

The Right Lead

Written by: Anna Harris

When I started Barrel Racing I thought that it was just about making a pattern around some over-sized tin cans. As I became more knowledgeable about what the sport was, I recognized that it takes more horsemanship than meets the eye.

Did you know that in the course of one run there are two lead changes? A lead change is determined by the forward leg when a horse is loping or running. Think of how a horses' hoof beat sounds. Try to make that rhythm with your own feet by going in a circle. The leg that goes out first is your leading foot. Take into consideration that at a full out run a horse can reach speeds around thirty five miles an hour. The right lead matters.

To change a horses' lead from right to left, tip the horses' nose to the right, then apply leg pressure to the right rib cage; that should cause the horses left shoulder to drive forward causing the leg to reach outward. You MUST do all this while the left leg is leaving the ground.

Just like following Jesus, it is not always going to be smooth ground, but you can bet your boots, that if you are committed, he will be with you the whole way keeping you in the correct lead.

The horse and rider have to be one so when the lead change needs to happen, they work together at that exact moment. Jesus knows at what moment we need a "lead change".

Commit yourself and every stride you take to Jesus.

Psalm 37:5 NKJV 5 "Commit your way to the Lord, Trust also in Him, And He shall bring it to pass.

Day 16

Miles from Nowhere

Written by: Jacob Harris

Photo Credit: Misty Crigger

Some of my fondest memories revolve around my family. Not just those that I live with, but also my Rodeo family. Down through the years we've traveled many miles together. Long hours spent driving all night to hit the next show.

We've seen freezing rain and heavy snow. They say that going through tough times together forms the strongest bond. I'm a firm believer in this as I sit and remember times long gone. I've been stuck on the side of a road 5 hours from home yet I was never alone, there's always been someone I can call, to help me back up when I fall.

Luke 10:30-37 "Jesus replied, "A man was going down from Jerusalem to Jericho, and he fell among robbers, who stripped him and beat him and departed, leaving him half dead. Now by chance a priest was going down that road, and when he saw him he passed by on the other side. So likewise a Levite, when he came to the place and saw him, passed by on the other side. But a Samaritan, as he journeyed, came to where he was, and when he saw him, he had compassion. He went to him and bound up his wounds, pouring on oil and wine. Then he set him on his own animal and brought him to an inn and took care of him."

Day 17

Harness Your Tongue

Written by: Anna Harris

"What you think about, you bring about!" "You are either speaking life or death". God wants us to live. The Bridle is used to direct a horse. It is a piece of equipment that includes the headstall and holds the bit that properly fits into the horse's mouth. This is attached to the reins, helping the rider communicate with the horse in which direction they should go. The weight, shape and material of the bit does make a difference in the response you will get. The bit should encourage your horse to respond to the lightest of touch and still be able to safely stop.

Being hurt, broken or treated unfairly can be like a harsh bit in your mouth. At first the pain is too powerful, blocking every turn. Pain that is allowed to linger will weaken your focus. A choice has to be made to not allow hurt to dictate your direction. If we give God free rein, he can take us to another level. Release brings freedom.

Not getting caught up in the barbwire of gossip, spreading the manure of half-truths or running people through the electric fence are a perfect way to let God lead you with a gentle tenderness. Release yourself from the pain and let God do the work. Just as a good horse hand recognizes the struggle of a bad bit, God does the same for us. Love never fails.

There are many scriptures in the bible about the power of the tongue. I encourage you to do your own research. For every negative you say or hear, think of three positives about the person or situation, (even if it does not pertain to you). This will train your mind to be more positive.

1 Peter 3:10 KJV " For, whoever would love life and see good days must keep their tongue

from evil and their lips from deceitful
speech."
Colossians 4:6 "Let your speech be always
with grace, and seasoned with salt, that ye
may know how ye ought to answer every
man.

Ephesians 4:29 KJV
"29 Let no corrupt communication proceed
out of your mouth, but that which is good to
the use of edifying, that it may minister grace
unto the hearers."

Proverbs 10:19 KJV
"19 In the multitude of words there wanteth
not sin: but he that refraineth his lips is
wise."

Proverbs 15:4 KJV
"4 A wholesome tongue is a tree of life: but
perverseness therein is a breach in the
spirit."

Proverbs 26:20 KJV
"20 Where no wood is, there the fire goeth
out: so where there is no talebearer, the strife
ceaseth."

Philippians 4:8 KJV
"8 Finally, brethren, whatsoever things are
true, whatsoever things are honest,
whatsoever things are just, whatsoever things
are pure, whatsoever things are lovely,
whatsoever things are of good report; if there
be any virtue, and if there be any praise,
think on these things."

Jeremiah 29:11 KJV
"11 For I know the thoughts that I think toward you, saith the Lord, thoughts of peace, and not of evil, to give you an expected end."

Wait upon the Lord

Written by: Emily Harris

Photo Credit: Sammy Crigger

If there was ever a time I had to be patient, it was waiting to be old enough to rodeo. You can start when you are three, but I had to wait until I was six and able to ride a horse. At the rodeo's I spent a lot of time sitting on the sidelines dreaming to participate with my friends in the Virginia Junior Rodeo Association.

To do my part, I would sell raffle tickets, pick up trash as well as cheer for my family and friends. During this time, I learned to wait upon the Lord. His timing is perfect. I will never forget my first run, on a borrowed horse. I appreciate getting to participate because I realize I have a rodeo family who is there for me and I know what it is like to wait for something you want really bad.

Mama says, "The lack of, is increase, because you realize the value of it more when you don't have it."

Isaiah 40:31 NKJV 31" But those who wait on the Lord, Shall renew their strength; They shall mount up with wings like eagles,
They shall run and not be weary, They shall walk and not faint."

Day 19

Help Meet

Photo: Credit: Faith Lawing

He clothes me in his love, protection and guidance; a true man of integrity. You can take this cowboy for his word. He is noble and worthy. I am honored to be his companion.

A Cowboy lives by a code that makes you feel safe, peaceful and just like being at home. He will never leave you behind and is always proud to have you by his side.

A true cowboy will have values that stand out from all the rest. He will ask your Daddy if he can spend time with you; reassuring him that he recognizes exactly how special you are. This may seem like a dying breed or a dream that may never come true, but if you seek your heavenly father, He will send the perfect cowboy for you.

At twilight when he tilts his hat and asks for a kiss remember he may not always be fancy but this is one cowboy you don't want to miss. God made woman from the life of man and with that creation was complete. Cowboys honor your bride. Cowgirls keep praying for your cowboy.

Genesis 2:18 KJV "18 And the Lord God said, It is not good that the man should be alone; I will make him a helpmeet for him."

Genesis 2:23 NKJV "This is now bone of my bones and flesh of my flesh; She shall be called Woman, Because she was taken out of Man."

Day 20

Treasures

Written by: Matthew Harris

Buckles are earned for all the Rodeo events; Team Roping, Bull Riding, Goat Tying, Barrels, Poles, Ribbon Roping, Chute Doggin, Trap Shooting, Light Rifle and also a buckle that is awarded to one cowboy or cowgirl called the Sportsmanship buckle . This is granted to a person that shows integrity, respect, and of course, sportsmanship. Not everyone receives a rodeo-issued buckle. It is an honor that must be earned.

The cowboy's award tells a story about his life. At a glance you will know what he is passionate about; where his time has been spent and what he treasures most.

As a cowboy myself I can tell you that we are proud to add this trophy to our wardrobe. Some may see a shiny piece of metal, but to a cowboy, it represents stories of the hardships and successes that our self, our horses and buddies have overcome. There have been relentless hours in the practice arena, freezing nights in the truck, broken down trailers, horses and at times pride. It is how you get up, that counts.

Coming out on top doesn't just happen. It takes true grit, determination and a mindset that you work harder to achieve what God has put on your heart. Every cowboy will tell you that he doesn't do it alone. He thanks God, his mount and competition, because one is only as good as those he competes with and against.

This is exactly like life. You have to be more determined than the obstacles you are up against knowing you come out stronger in the end. You do this by continuing to get up and get back on. You cannot always decide the stock you ride, or who you compete with but you can choose how you handle yourself.

When you walk with the Lord, his word covers your body. You are an example of his hard work and dedication. Who you are is God's trophy, his shiny buckle. I encourage you to think about what your treasures are and the effort you are putting into them.

Matthew 6:21 NKJV 21" For where your treasure is, there your heart will be also."

Day 21

The Life He Leads

Written by Jacob Harris

Photo Credit: Taylor Lester Photography

When you first see him, you may wonder what it's like to live the life he leads. From sun up to sun down, he tends to the needs of those that depend on him. No matter the weather, season or holiday, he simply does the things he has been called to do; because a working man is all he ever was.

The reason behind this, most just don't understand. His story is told in the calluses on his hands. He works all day until the job is done, pausing not often, to take time for fun.

Through the years he has seen it all, from the flowers in the spring to the colors in the fall. He has watched his good friends answer their master call, never to return to the men riding tall. So if you truly wish to know what his life is like, saddle up and ride with him for one day and night.

When you trust the Lord with all your heart, he will lead and equip you with all you need.

Exodus 15:2 KJV "The LORD is my strength and song, and he has become my salvation: he is my God, and I will prepare him an habitation; my father's God, and I will exalt him."

Day 22

The Difference of a Father

Photo: Credit: Tiffany Baird

I love how in this photo the father is trying to keep up with his son. Or maybe he is letting him lead the way. The smile says it all, "success." It reminds me of how our heavenly father must feel when we make it through those difficult times with a smile on our face. You know the struggles I am talking about; when you put fear to the side, face the unknown, mount up, get a grip and enjoy the ride. The odds may be against you and three to four times your size, but there is just something in you that say's, "Hang on.

Don't quit!" No matter the outcome, your Papa is there to help carry your load. The wisdom of a father knows when to let his child stroll ahead and when he needs him by his side with a supporting hand on his shoulder.

What a father teaches his son makes a difference in his life. It is his job to be involved and prepare his children to be ready. A father creates the atmosphere based on the foundation that he builds his family on.   It is the father's duty to tend to his family on behalf of God. You need to know who your children's friends are and how they are spending their time.

Your children will learn how to handle a win and loss by your example. Your kids will have the favor that you teach them, to have the faith for.

DO NOT MISS THE IMPORTANT SEASON OF FATHERHOOD.

Proverbs 13:1-12 NKJV 1" A wise son heeds his father's instruction, But a scoffer does not listen to rebuke. 2 A man shall eat well by the fruit of his mouth, But the soul of the unfaithful feeds on violence. 3 He who guards his mouth preserves his life, But he who opens wide his lips shall have destruction. 4 The soul of a lazy man desires, and has nothing; But the soul of the diligent shall be made rich. 5 A righteous man hates lying, But a wicked man is loathsome and comes to shame. 6 Righteousness guards him whose way is blameless, But wickedness overthrows the sinner. 7 There is one who makes himself rich, yet has nothing; And one who makes himself poor, yet has great riches. 8 The ransom of a man's life is his riches, But the poor does not hear rebuke. 9 The light of the righteous rejoices, But the lamp of the wicked will be put out. 10 By pride comes nothing but strife, But with the well-advised is wisdom. 11 Wealth gained by dishonesty will be diminished, But he who gathers by labor will increase. 12 Hope deferred makes the heart sick, But when the desire comes, it is a tree of life."

Day 23

Cowboys

Written by: Jacob Harris

Photo Credit: Chelsey Carico

Cowboys don't just chase the white lines to the next rodeo. They put God first, family and livestock second and they live their life working until the job is done.

They tend to their horses, cattle, farming, ranching and anything that comes their way.

A cowboy will look you eye to eye and say what needs to be said, even if it isn't what you want to hear. He makes a deal with a firm handshake and his word and expects the same from you. Cowboy's and their families know that others depend on them and you can bet your boots, they are giving life their all. There is no sit back and wait for someone else to do it or wait until the mood hits.

Honor, pride, dedication and integrity are a cowboy's way of life. You can take him for his word. He knows who he is and who he wants to be. Most will probably have the same answer. "I want to be proud of the man I am and when I lay my head down at night, be proud of what I have accomplished. When I search my soul, I want to know I am leaving a legacy of faith that my word and life stood on."

Matthew 6:33 NKJV 33 "But seek first the kingdom of God and His righteousness, and all these things shall be added to you."

Day 24

Luke Crigger

Written by: Matthew Harris

Photo Credit: Sammy Crigger

Luke Crigger and I have shared many amazing experiences along with horses and gear over the past 7 going on 8 years.
We have celebrated and simply said, "You will get it next time bud."

When I first started rodeo I only competed in sheep riding due to the fact that I didn't have a horse. Luke noticed how much I wanted to compete in goat tying so he offered me a chance to borrow his horse named Susie. I would be competing against Luke, but he still helped me out. We have had an unbreakable friendship since.

For almost an entire season, I borrowed Susie. Since then our families have been on many journeys, National's and fishing trips together, making memories of the best kind.

Like most young cowboys, I decided that I wanted to try my hand at Team Roping. I started heeling on my brother's horse but after about three rodeos in, it was obvious, the horse and I didn't click at all for this event, but my dreams weren't shattered. Luke stepped up again and let me borrow his horse named Matt for the next 9 rodeos, until the end of the season.

Once summer came and the VJRA ended The Crigger's invited us to an open rodeo near their house. When we arrived Luke explained how Ol' Matt was mine! He just up and gave me his horse!

We had a rodeo in Perry Georgia but due to my large family of 9 we would have had to take two vehicles. Luke came along asking if my brother and I wanted to make the 10 hour trip with them. This is what family is about, being there for one another. Luke's got my back and I hope he knows; I have his. Luke puts others before himself and puts his heart into all he does.

Matthew 7:12 NKJV 12 "Therefore, whatever you want men to do to you, do also to them, for this is the Law and the Prophets."

Day 25

Ol Gus

Written by: Jacob Harris

Photo Credit: Gus Kluts

First time I laid eyes on Ol 'Gus, we were throwing my beat up rope saddle on his mount. Our truck was down and I had entered an open rodeo about 2 hours away in my hometown, Dublin, Virginia.
We made a few calls to some close friends trying to see if we could borrow a horse for

me to rope on that night, but had little to no luck. So our friends got on the horn with Gus. He picked up on the 3rd or 4th ring and agreed to let me use his horse if I could make it there on time. So we threw my ropes in the car and away we went down the interstate, trying to make a 2 hour trip in one.

We pulled in about three minutes before the 1st team was supposed to rope their steer. Gus was standing there at the gate with his horse in one hand and a parking pass in the other. As we piled out of the car, he threw the parking pass in the dash and said, "Hi, I'm Gus, this is my horse and you're the 1st team out."

Now before I go on let me paint you a picture of Gus. Are you ready? Close your eyes and picture Jack Elam. I'm just kidding, "Sorry Gus, I had to pick on you a little bit." He looks nothing like that. Gus is about 6'2, 170 pounds. Now me, I'm a little feller. I'm about 5' nothing and 80 pounds soaking wet; so when we threw my saddle up on his pony it didn't fit right at all.

Now keep in mind that we still are running against the clock. My saddle was pinching the fire out of his horses' withers. So Gus makes a b-line to his trailer, throws his rig up on Ol' Grey's back and runs over to the roping boxes. I clambered up in the new saddle and found just how much longer his legs were than mine! When I looked down to see how much they needed to come up they just as well been a mile and a 1/2 away because there was no way in heck I could have reached them with my feet. My legs would have had to have grown about two feet. Gus knew as well as I did, that wasn't gonna happen anytime soon.   So Gus whipped out his knife and started punching holes in his stirrup leathers.

About the time he finished the last hole, we heard my name called over the loudspeaker. I loped his horse one lap around the arena and backed into the heel box.

I ended up missing my shot on the corner and went home empty handed with one exception. I gained the friendship of Gus Klutz. Due to his outgoing personality and dedication to the rodeo community, not only was I able to compete but also learned an important lesson. No matter what, kindness to strangers goes a long way. I appreciate You Gus.

You'd think the story would end there, but it doesn't.   Several hours into our trip, on our way back home from our most recent rodeo in Perry, GA, we had pulled over on the side of the interstate to check our trailer. Guess who pulled alongside us asking if we needed a hand? You guessed it, Good Ol' Gus.

Determination is proposing to accomplish God's goals in God's time regardless of the opposition.

"I have fought a good fight, I have finished my course, I have kept the faith: Henceforth there is laid up for me a crown of righteousness....."
II Timothy 4:7,8

Day 26

Eli Prince

Written by: Jacob Harris

When a group of cowboys and cowgirls come together, chances are someone will be in need of a prayer or two for something! Like Colossians 4:2, we believe in staying prayed up, continuing in prayer.

It makes no difference if the prayer is for thanksgiving or a covering of protection for our competitors and the stock; it is who is called on to lead us in prayer. It has to be a person of good character that not only knows the Code of the Cowboy, but lives it daily. His word has to mean something and he realizes his actions speak for the man he is.

Eli Prince is just that Cowboy. When multi-state rodeos take place he is the one that his peers turn to for direction. When as a whole we go before the Lord submitting prayers and are at a loss for words, through tears and faith, Eli leads to the cross; somehow finding the life giving, peace filling words to humbly speak before God.

It takes integrity, doing what is right, even when no one is looking, to be a good leader; putting your best boot forward, in and out of the arena, center stage or behind closed doors.

I know many others will agree that Eli Prince is definitely, "That Cowboy." He believes in being kind to others, doing what's right and always giving your best.

Eli,

May you continue to always stand firm in your faith, have the wisdom to know there is so much to learn and the love that you never forget where you came from or who you belong to. May your boot print continue to lead the way because those little cowboys want to grow up to be, "Just like YOU someday."

Colossians 4:2-6 2 "Devote your selves to prayer, being watchful and thankful. 3 And pray for us, too, that God may open a door for our message, so that we may proclaim the mystery of Christ, for which I am in chains. 4 Pray that I may proclaim it clearly, as I should. 5 Be wise in the way you act toward outsiders; make the most of every opportunity. 6 Let your conversation be always full of grace, seasoned with salt, so that you may know how to answer everyone."

Day 27

Jacob Crigger

Written by: Jacob Harris

Photo Credit: Sammy Crigger

Jacob Crigger and I have been friends for a long while now and through the years he has proven that he is one of those people that YOU can count on.

No matter the circumstance he and his family are ever present in my time of need. I remember on one such occasion we had a big out of state rodeo and once again our truck was in the shop. (I know when you travel as much as we do there is bound to be vehicle trouble, but I swear it seems like ours spend just as much time being worked on as they do on the road). Anyway, The Crigger Family came to my aid. They not only turned their rig around to come pick me up but also allowed me to use their horses in order to compete.

Shortly after we pulled into the rodeo, Crigger and I went up to check the draw in the main arena. Surprisingly neither of us were up that night so we decided to ride the horses around the grounds and let them get use to their surroundings and so that I would have at least one ride under my belt before the performance on Saturday. Well we rode until it got dark, put the horses away and went to bed around 10:00 p.m. The next morning before the performance, we ate breakfast and to got ready to rope.

There was just one person in between Crigger and myself, so right after Crigger roped I had to jump on his calf horse. I ended up winning the first go with a 9.3 and missing my second calf on Sunday. Without friends like these there is no way that I would have been able to compete in his great sport.

It is not just the sacrifice YOU make for YOURSELF, but the sacrifice that others make for YOU.

Jacob not only loaned me his horse and rope to compete against him, he coached me on what I needed to do. We aren't just friends, we are truly brothers. He puts his best boot forward by helping his com padres do the same. Cowboy strong.

Roman's 15:2 NKJV 2" Let each of us please his neighbor for his good, leading to edification."

Day 28

Lauren Parent

Written by: Anna Harris

The first time I met Lauren Parent, we were working. Both of us had volunteered to hang the Associations'

Sponsor Banners on the panels of the arena Ever since, she has been an amazing leader and the truest of true friend.

Lauren never says a negative word about a rough rodeo or other people. She is always encouraging others to keep trying their best and to never give up. This cowgirl is the first one you can call on for prayer or to lend a helping hand, no matter what the task is. Catching your horse, changing saddles, loaning you her boots or spurs, helping you watch your siblings, whatever YOU need, she is there. She has a keen eye and her knowledge of horses are a few of her many attributes.

Rodeo is a tough, competitive sport, and each run does not always go as planned. No matter the outcome, Lauren leaves the arena with a smile and no doubt praying for the next cowgirl to have a successful run. One of the great things about our rodeo family, we know what that a success feels like and wish every kid in the world could experience it at least one time in their life.

To the "rest of my life rodeo sister", Lauren Parent, Thank YOU for being one of the most humble, peaceful people I know. The miles of laughter we have shared have blessed not only my life, but my family's as well. I am so excited for Nationals this year and all that we will experience.   Best of luck my sweet friend.
Love,
Anna Harris

Philippians 2:1-5 "So if there is any encouragement in Christ, any comfort from love, any participation in the Spirit, any affection and sympathy, complete my joy by being of the same mind, having the same love, being in full accord and of one mind. Do nothing from rivalry or conceit, but in humility count others more significant than yourselves. Let each of you look not only to his own interests, but also to the interests of others. Have this mind among yourselves, which is yours in Christ Jesus."

Day 29

The Brown Boys

Written by: Matthew Harris

Photo Credit: Theresa Brown

Hugh, Jeremy and Paul Brown are amazing friends, actually more like brothers to me. The reason I say this is because they may be competing against me, and I them, we still strive to help each other out. I have been competing in rodeo with the Brown Brothers for seven years and value the knowledge that the boys share, passed from generation to generation.

Like their dad and his dad before them, they have been inspired and infected with the love for horses. They go out of their way to teach me and our buddies the various techniques for the events we compete in such as, Team Roping, calf roping, tie down, goat tying, and in our younger years, barrels, poles. Their dad has taught them to know that it won't be easy. You have to be dedicated and work hard. Be humble, pay attention to detail and all the little things because that is how success comes.

I've seen these three boys put a saddle on the horse, compete, then as soon as they're done help change the stirrup length in the arena just so someone could compete against them on their horse. An amazing thing about them is that if somehow you fall on your face in the arena, they don't laugh until they know you are ok. Over some concession fries they tell you how funny it was.

The Brown Brother's gave a presentation to a group of school kids about the Virginia Rodeo Association. They put together a PowerPoint presentation on all the events that they compete in. The class followed the brothers outside where they gave them their old cowboy hats, ropes and taught them roping techniques.

After all the excitement and answering many questions the Brown Brothers left these kids with an amazing memory, planted some seeds and dreams and left them brochures about the Virginia High School Rodeo Association.

These three boys are a fine example of leadership, honesty and integrity.

The Brown brothers definitely put their Best Boot Forward and help others do the same and I'm sure the other families agree.

Luke 6:38 "Give, and it will be given to you. Good measure, pressed down, shaken together, running over, will be put into your lap. For with the measure you use it will be measured back to you."

Day 30

This Ol' Hat

Written by: Jacob Harris

This old hat might look a little rough but to me it seems pretty dang tough. A lifetime of memories gathered in one place, leaving no room for empty space. Every bend or twist, busted stitch and splash of mud, has a story to tell if one only pauses long enough to see. This Ol' hat wasn't put through hell, but has lived a full life just the same you and me.

It's been a loyal companion for many years, seen many places and countless tears.

Some on the face of the man he serves, but the most in the eyes of those that observe the freedom he has as he roams the range, untouched by man, wild and untamed.

Through this life and on to the next this Ol' hat will be put to the test, rain wind, snow and hail, one never can tell. There's one thing left I'd like to say before you go on your way. In life, there are many troubles and as time goes on, those will only double, but do not worry friend for that is true but this old hat will help you through.

Isaiah 58:11 KJV "11" And the Lord shall guide thee continually, and satisfy thy soul in drought, and make fat thy bones: and thou shalt be like a watered garden, and like a spring of water, whose waters fail not."

Photo Credits

Carrie Stanovick - Heartland Retrievers

Chelsey Carico- Photos by Chelsey & Co.,
Collection Carico, Chance Carico Music

Faith Lawing

Gus Kluts Circle K Performance Horses

Page Graves- Walnut Creek Farm
walnutcreekfarm@msn.com
Pleasure & Performance, Licensed & Bonded

"Pops" Joe Smith

Sammy Crigger & Misty Crigger
Hope and Faith Equine Therapy

Taylor Lester Photography

Theresa Brown- Hoof and Paw Veterinary

Tiffany Baird - Images by Tiffany
tiffany@imagesbytiffany.net

Made in the USA
Middletown, DE
07 August 2020